T0016102

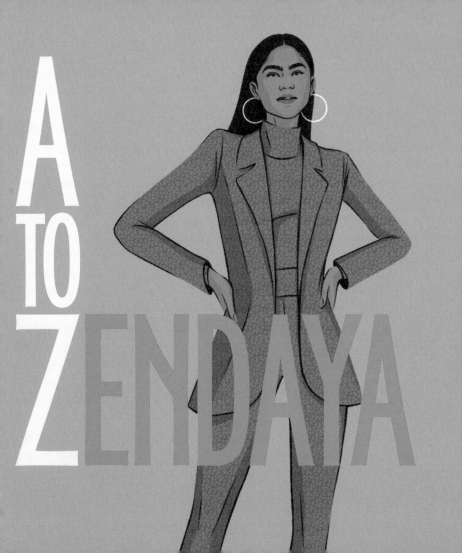

A TO ZENDAYA

A TO ZENDAYA

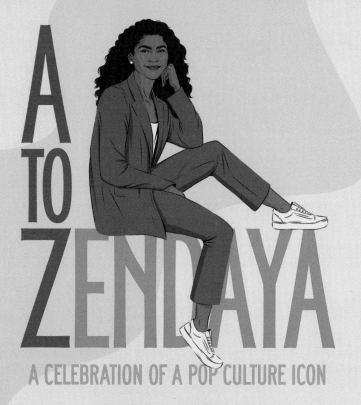

A CELEBRATION OF A POP CULTURE ICON

Written by Satu Hämeenaho-Fox
Illustrated by Sarah Madden

INTRODUCTION

What does it mean to be a star? Once upon a time, celebrities could stay in their bubble, do their work, and expect the praise from fans to roll in. Nowadays, it's harder to thread the needle: they need to be glamorous but relatable, talented but also business-minded, ready to play the media game while keeping closely in touch with their fans. Only a handful of people can finesse this, and that is what makes Zendaya a true star of our time.

Overcoming the prejudice against Disney stars and child stars in general, Zendaya has proved she can entertain in comedies and also blow us away in intense dramas. Maybe you saw her for the first time glittering darkly as Rue in *Euphoria*, or being a ray of sunshine in *K.C. Undercover* or *Shake it Up*. Maybe you could relate to the dry wit of MJ in the Spider-Man movies, or perhaps it was one of her unique, boundary-breaking red carpet looks that drew you in. Zendaya is here for the binge-watchers, the movie buffs, and the fashionistas.

On the topic of style, Zendaya is beautiful, but she's not here to appeal to the male gaze. Working closely with her incredible stylist, Law Roach, she creates outfits that accentuate her unique beauty and break through the noise. From a chrome breastplate fitted to her figure, to the way she weaves webs into her Spider-Man premiere outfits, she's doing fashion thoughtfully, using her brain as well as her body to tell a story.

The thing about Zendaya is that she lets herself be all the Zendayas. She's not faking it on the red carpet—she loves it. And then she loves going home to get into her sweats. She's poised and professional, but she won't hesitate to call out injustice when she sees it, whether it will help her image or not. A self-confident, radiant young Black woman who works towards justice for all and does it while serving looks? That's the star we've been waiting for.

Zendaya, a big believer in staying true to yourself, says, "It's important to find out who you are and love who you are. Everyone has a journey." Although she shines bright, we have barely scratched the surface of what she can achieve: this is just the beginning of her journey.

A

IS FOR

ALL ABOUT ZENDAYA

Full name: Zendaya Maree Stoermer Coleman

Education: High School graduate

Birthday: 1 September
Year born: 1996
Birthplace: Oakland, California

Mom: Claire Marie Stoermer
Dad: Kazembe Coleman
Siblings: Brothers Austin and Julien, and sisters Katianna, AnnaBella, and Kaylee

Favorite movies: *A Wrinkle in Time, Get Out, If Beale Street Could Talk, Superbad,* and *Interstellar*

Shoe size: US 9
Height: 5 ft 10 in

ANXIETY

Like many of us, Zendaya is prone to anxiety. "Stress and anxiety is a constant factor in my life due to my work and how tough I am on myself," she says. She hasn't totally cured herself of the feeling but tries to manage it with activities that make her happy, like painting, journaling, and being outside in nature. Her advice is not to suffer in silence: "there's nothing wrong with working on yourself and dealing with those things with someone who can help you, someone who can talk to you."

A WHITE LIE

In 2018, it was announced that Zendaya was producing and starring in the movie *A White Lie*, along with actor and producer Reese Witherspoon. Based on a true story, it's about an African-American woman who passes as white to attend university in the 1890s. The movie has been "in development" ever since, so sadly it may never happen.

A IS ALSO FOR...

AVOCADO PASTA

Zendaya is not a whizz in the kitchen, and was even rushed to hospital with a minor injury after slicing her finger while cooking ("See now... this is why I don't cook," she said on Instagram). The one recipe she has mentioned cooking from scratch is pasta with a sauce made from avocado. Proud Zendaya said the unusual dish was "super easy, minimal ingredients, and it was freaking delicious."

BLACK LIVES MATTER

Zendaya is a proud supporter of the Black Lives Matter movement, a campaign that seeks to highlight racism, discrimination, and racial inequality experienced by Black people. In 2020, she went on protest marches, cementing her role "as a leader amongst young people" and showing that "you're not too young to make a difference."

As well as taking to the streets and speaking up in interviews whenever she gets the chance, Zendaya has platformed more experienced activists within the movement. She invited Patrisse Cullors, BLM co-founder, to take over her Instagram, and spoke to her for *InStyle* magazine. Zendaya said, "I didn't know what I could do to help. And that's when I reach out to people like you. Because at the end of the day, I'm just an actress, you know? And I don't pretend to be anything other than that. If I don't know something, then I ask people who are actually on the front lines doing the work."

As part of her 2022 Emmy Award acceptance speech, Zendaya used the moment to express her support for community organizers and committed activists, saying "I just want to say to all my peers out there doing the work in the streets, I see you, I admire you, I thank you."

B IS ALSO FOR...
BLACK-ISH

Zendaya made a cameo in beloved sitcom *Black-ish*, playing daughter Zoey's friend Resheida. She gets involved in dad Dre's scheme to start a "Daddy's Day" to help fathers get the recognition they deserve. It's a shame Resheida only appeared once as she is a hilarious foil to Dre, eventually becoming his stand-in daughter for the Daddy's Day pitch.

BAD BLOOD

One of the biggest singles from Taylor Swift's 2015 album *1989* was "Bad Blood", featuring Kendrick Lamar. Among the 17 (!) celebrity cameos in the video was Zendaya, playing Cut Throat, an assassin who pins an unlucky teddy bear to the wall with a dagger. Zendaya featured in a classic music video 'walking away from explosion' moment with Taylor, who she called a "genius."

BARBIE

A custom Barbie™ doll was created to celebrate Zendaya's 2015 Oscars red carpet look. A clearly touched Zendaya appreciated that the makers "took time with the hair, because obviously the hair was so important" (see page 62 for the backstory). She added, "When I was little I couldn't find a Barbie that looked like me, my... how times have changed."

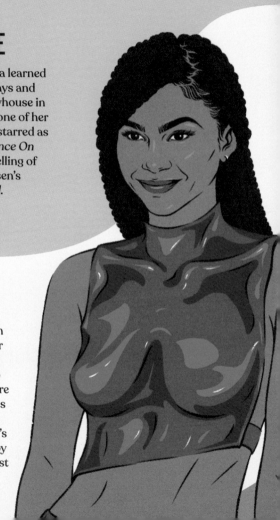

BERKELEY PLAYHOUSE

Before her TV days, Zendaya learned acting by appearing in plays and musicals. The Berkeley Playhouse in California was the scene of one of her earliest performances. She starred as the young Ti Moune in *Once On This Island*, a musical retelling of Hans Christian Andersen's *The Little Mermaid*.

BREASTPLATE

Although Zendaya had been wearing incredible looks for years, her style icon status was confirmed by the deep pink breastplate that she wore to the Critics' Choice Awards in 2020. It was a moment. 3D-printed so it fit Zendaya's torso exactly, the garment by designer Tom Ford would cost you $15,000 to buy.

B IS ALSO FOR...

BETWEEN U
AND ME

Zendaya's book *Between U and Me: How to rock your tween years with style and confidence* is a guide for facing the tricky years where you're not a girl, not yet a woman. Written and illustrated by Zendaya, she gives practical advice that actually applies to people of any age, including how to make friends. She advises readers to seek out people you have things in common with: "Sign up for activities or after-school clubs so you can meet people who share your interests. I did a lot of hanging with the kids who liked performing and acting."

IS FOR

CHALLENGERS

Zendaya began filming the movie *Challengers* in 2022. She plays Tashi, a tennis coach whose tennis player husband (played by Broadway star Mike Faist) isn't performing well. She makes him enter a 'Challenger' tournament (a competition for lower-performing players) where he comes up against her ex, played by Josh O'Connor from hit Netflix drama *The Crown*.

Challengers is directed by *Call Me By Your Name* director Luca Guadagnino, but unlike that angsty, slow-burn love story famous for its Timmy Chalamet performance, he says this movie is a "fizzy, sexy" romantic comedy.

Over the past decade, the Williams sisters have helped to transform the image of tennis from a rather stuffy, exclusive game to an elite sport that powerful women can excel in, including women of color.

With Zendaya as star and producer, plus costumes from cutting-edge designer JW Anderson, the project is an all-round masterpiece.

C IS ALSO FOR...

CINDERELLA

For the Met Gala 2019 (theme: "Camp: Notes on Fashion"), Zendaya referenced her Disney background by dressing as Cinderella. "I'ma be honest with you, this Met stressed me out," Zendaya later admitted to *Vogue*. "I got there and [the dress] wasn't ready." But with the hard work of the Tommy Hilfiger design team, and a wave of a wand from her fairy godmother (stylist Law Roach), her blue, puff-sleeved dress literally lit up the pink carpet using LED technology.

COLORISM

As a light-skinned Black woman, Zendaya has spoken out about the privilege she has compared to those with darker skin: "Can I honestly say that I've had to face the same racism and struggles as a woman with darker skin? No, I cannot." Acknowledging that she is given opportunities in acting because of the way she looks, she said, "I am Hollywood's acceptable version of a Black girl and that has to change."

COBWEBS

Some of Zendaya's wittiest looks have been the cobweb-covered outfits she wore on the promo tour for Spider-Man. For the London premiere of *No Way Home*, she wore a look by British fashion house Alexander McQueen: an oversized gray blazer with crystal cobwebs on the shoulders and crystal cobweb tights. She even wore diamond-studded cobweb earrings.

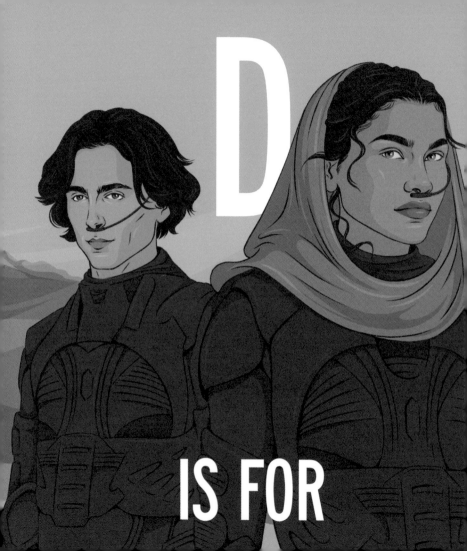

D

IS FOR

DUNE

The 2021 sci-fi blockbuster *Dune* is a gorgeous, slow-paced exploration of destiny and Timothée Chalamet's bone structure, set on a desert planet where intergalactic houses fight for a precious substance called "the spice". For seven brief minutes, Zendaya plays Chani, a girl from the planet's indigenous Fremen people. For most of the movie we see her in visions of the future and guess that she is going to be Paul's (Timothée's) love interest.

When Chani eventually shows up, it's to tell Paul he's definitely going to be killed in the hand-to-hand combat he is about to engage in. No spoilers for the outcome of that battle, but there is a *Dune: Part 2*, scheduled for release in the winter of 2023. The movie's director Denis Villeneuve has reassured fans that Chani will become a bigger part of the story, saying, "For Zendaya, I will say Part One was a promise."

A-grade actors such as Florence Pugh and *Elvis* star Austin Butler have also joined the cast of *Dune 2*, making it almost *too* full of incredible talent.

D IS ALSO FOR...

DAD

Zendaya's father, Kazembe Ajamu Coleman, also acts as her manager. A former teacher like her mom, he moved to LA to help Zendaya at the start of her career. Far from the stereotype of a pushy stage parent, Kazembe encourages his daughter to be strong and independent, saying, "I want Zendaya to speak for herself."

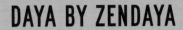

DAYA BY ZENDAYA

Starting her own fashion line in 2016 was a logical step for Zendaya. She took a hands-on approach to the business, even giving it one of her nicknames, Daya. With inclusive sizing and an affordable price range, Daya was a fun, if brief, project—Zendaya closed the brand in 2018.

DANCING WITH THE STARS

Zendaya was only 16 when she competed in *Dancing with the Stars*. She and her partner Valentin received the first perfect scores of the competition with their Argentine tango (dancing to music by Hans Zimmer, who would later provide the soundtrack to her movie *Dune*), and went on to place second, beaten to the mirrorball trophy by Kellie Pickler and Derek Hough.

23

DRIVING

Zendaya has many talents, but sadly driving isn't one of them. She once got her Lexus stuck half-on/half-off a curb and she had to call a breakdown service (although she claimed it was the fault of the "big ass curb"). In spite of this, Zendaya owns at least four other luxury cars, including a Range Rover.

DARNELL APPLING

Zendaya met her assistant and friend Darnell on the set of *K.C. Undercover*, and he now organizes her life for her. He can be spotted in her *Vogue* "73 Questions" interview making lemonade, or taking her to the hospital when she cut her finger while cooking. They are so close, she calls him her "big brother."

D IS ALSO FOR...

DIG DOWN DEEPER

One of the best songs in Zendaya's Disney catalog, "Dig Down Deeper" is a gardening-themed deep cut. Released way back in 2011 as part of the soundtrack for the animated movie *Pixie Hollow Games*, it's infectious and has a positive message about digging within yourself to nurture inner strength. Zendaya wears all the pink and purple sequins in the accompanying music video.

E
IS FOR

EUPHORIA

With its dark themes of addiction, abuse, and manipulation among a group of teens, *Euphoria* could be a huge downer. It's rescued from being totally depressing by glorious performances from Zendaya and her cast-mates.

Zendaya plays narrator Rue, a complex, intriguing character who liberated Zendaya's acting skills and allowed people to see her in a new light. Critic Rebecca Nicholson described it as "a truly astonishing, mesmerizing performance, upending every expectation of what she could do."

The show is controversial for its candid portrayal of teenage drug use, but Zendaya says her aim in playing Rue is to help those who are struggling with addiction: "Our show is in no way a moral tale to teach people how to live their life or what they should be doing. If anything, the feeling behind *Euphoria* ... is to hopefully help people feel a little bit less alone in their experience and their pain."

Euphoria is HBO's second most-watched show of the past 20 years, beaten only by *Game of Thrones*.

ECZEMA

As well as suffering from acne (like most of us at some point!) Zendaya has eczema, which can make your skin itchy and dry. Her advice is not to treat your skin too aggressively: "... when I start to apply too many layers of things and too many different masks ... I break out or I get an eczema flare up. So I got to keep it simple." She refuses to be pressured into covering up her imperfections, stating, "I'm very proud of my skin and my face."

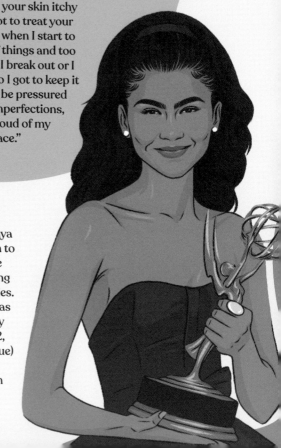

EMMY AWARDS

In 2020, aged just 24, Zendaya became the youngest woman to win the coveted Primetime Emmy Award for Outstanding Lead Actress in a Drama Series. Her award for playing Rue was one of three Emmys won by *Euphoria* that year. In 2022, the award went to her (and Rue) once again, making her the youngest actress to win an Emmy twice.

E IS ALSO FOR...

EYEBROWS

Zendaya openly admits she has an obsession with her eyebrows, which is fair because they are perfection. While she takes time to keep them looking their best, she also advises not doing too much, which anyone who has ever over-plucked or over-filled will understand. "Go with the natural idea of your eyebrows because really the way your eyebrows go in is the way that they're supposed to be."

F IS FOR

FEMINIST

FEMINIST

Zendaya fights for her characters to be more than the usual female stereotypes, saying that she often gets sent roles that "seem kind of like the same person over and over and over again." Pushing back on "one-dimensional" women onscreen, she demanded that K.C. from *K.C. Undercover* "be able to do everything that a guy can do."

Her feminism is about more than portraying kick-ass girls, however. As ambitious as she is, Zendaya knows that we can only make progress if we work together rather than just hustling to advance our own interests: "... we're so much more powerful together ... when we look out for each other, when we uplift each other, when we protect each other."

As a Black woman, Zendaya also knows how some voices are listened to more than others, encouraging us all to show solidarity to "women that look like you, women who don't look like you, women whose experiences are different than you. That means Black women, that means trans women, that means all women." A true feminist icon.

F IS ALSO FOR...

FRENEMIES

Zendaya and her Disney work wife Bella Thorne appeared together in the 2012 TV movie *Frenemies*. The storyline actually mirrors their real-life relationship. Zendaya plays Halley, who is pitted against Bella's Avalon to become the top editor of website GeeklyChic (Halley is the geek, Avalon the chic). Of course, by the end they become BFFs.

FIRST LOVE

Zendaya's first love lasted from 2012 to 2016 and sadly the breakup "wasn't a good ending". Instead of moping, though, Zendaya made herself move on: "I got rid of old text messages, pictures and their clothing I still had." She didn't name her ex but sent them the message, via a *Vogue* interview, that the breakup was "the dumbest decision of your life."

FASHION AWARD

The Council of Fashion Designers of America's coveted Fashion Icon Award went to Zendaya in 2021. She wore a red bandeau top and puffed skirt by Chinese-American designer Vera Wang to accept her award, which was previously won by the likes of Lady Gaga and supermodel Naomi Campbell. In her speech, she shouted out "smaller brands that dressed me before anyone else did."

FUTURE SHOCK

Adding hip-hop to her impressive portfolio of dance skills, Zendaya joined the Future Shock Oakland troupe at just eight years old. The program gives dance mentoring to under-17s to encourage "teamwork, respect, and positive self-expression." Zendaya, who seems to be able to dance any style, brought her natural swagger to the complex routines.

FASHION IS MY KRYPTONITE

A Kesha-style song on the most important topic in all of music—looking good in the club— "Fashion Is My Kryptonite" is a duet with Zendayaverse hero Bella Thorne. Recorded for the "Made in Japan" episode of Disney Channel sitcom *Shake It Up* (see page 95 for more), there was also a video where the girls dance and rap in a fantastical garden full of cute outfits.

F IS ALSO FOR...

FAR FROM HOME

MJ gets a lot more screen time in the second Spider-Man movie, *Far From Home*, wears more feminist t-shirts ("VOTES FOR WOMEN"), and delivers more dry quips. She confirms the suspicions that began in *Homecoming* and confronts Peter about his secret identity. In a very awkward and wholesome moment, they finally share their first kiss.

IS FOR

THE GREATEST SHOWMAN

With music from the songwriters behind *Dear Evan Hansen*, 2017's musical *The Greatest Showman* was the perfect showcase for Zendaya's singing and dancing skills. Hugh Jackman plays P.T. Barnum, the kind of guy who is always about to "make it big" with an unlikely money-making scheme. He finally finds success by starting a circus filled with talented performers, from Lettie the bearded lady to professional acrobats. Zendaya plays Anne, a trapeze artist who captivates love interest Philip, played by movie musical legend Zac Efron.

The Greatest Showman has catchy songs and a charismatic cast, but what made it a hit was its theme of empowering people with physical differences, who were shunned in the 19th century and called 'freaks'. The racism Anne faces from Philip's snobby parents shows another type of prejudice. While she gives a touching performance in her scenes outside the circus tent, the standout moments are Zendaya's trapeze sequences, cleverly woven into the romance storyline. The movie was a smash, making more than $430 million worldwide.

G IS ALSO FOR...

GENESIS TRAMAINE

Zendaya was never going to tack up an old poster on her bedroom wall—her beautiful home demands fine art. She has publicly stated her appreciation for New Jersey-based artist Genesis Tramaine, who creates abstract portraits in bold colors. No word on whether Tramaine has painted Zendaya's portrait, but she owns at least one painting by the artist.

GARDENIA

Zendaya's favorite flowers are gardenias, which have lots of white petals and a delicate scent. In fact, she loves them so much she not only has them growing in her garden, but once bought ten gardenia-scented candles to make sure every corner of her home would be filled with their floral fragrance.

GRYFFINDOR

Harry Potter super-fan Zendaya revealed that her Hogwarts house would be Gryffindor because she's "always loved lions." In fact, she even went to the Harry Potter Warner Bros. Studio Tour in London for her 22nd birthday and wore a burgundy and yellow pullover to show her affiliation. Courageous Gryffindor Zendaya says she finds the movies "calming" and has them on constant repeat.

HOMECOMING

Homecoming, the first standalone Spider-Man movie in the Marvel Cinematic Universe (MCU), found superhero Peter Parker at high school, attending classes and doing completely normal extracurriculars like academic decathlon. His team-mates include best friend Ned, captain (and crush) Liz, and a laid-back loner with a dry sense of humor called Michelle, played by Zendaya.

Peter is convinced he is going to become a full-time Avenger any day now, so he starts to flake on decathlon, vanishing during an important competition to prevent the sale of dangerous weapons. His absence raises Michelle's suspicions, but she doesn't say anything—yet.

Michelle starts the movie admitting she has no friends, but grows closer to Peter and the other decathletes, and is even named captain when Liz is forced to move schools. Although Zendaya's character isn't closely based on the MJ of the comic books, the nickname reveal is a hint that she may become more central to Peter's story.

H IS ALSO FOR...

HOLLYWOOD RECORDS

Like many other Disney stars, Zendaya was signed to the studio's own Hollywood Records. The record label has represented singers from Miley Cyrus and the Jonas Brothers to rising stars like *High School Musical: The Musical* performer Sabrina Carpenter. Zendaya tweeted that signing her record contract was an "epic moment in my life."

HULA DANCING

Zendaya is a trained hula dancer. She studied the traditional dance style for two years at the Academy of Hawaiian Arts in Oakland, California. Videos of her performing hula show an eight-year-old Zendaya nailing the graceful, swaying hip movements. Her top hula tip? "Keep your shoulders straight without moving."

HUNTER SCHAFER

Zendaya and co-star Hunter Schafer shared an intense romantic storyline in Seasons One and Two of *Euphoria*. As a result, Hunter says that Zendaya is the fellow actor she is the closest to, while Zendaya attributes their bond to the way "[Hunter] has seen me in every form, the worst, the best, and vice versa."

I

IS
FOR

INFLUENCE

TIME magazine's annual list of the world's "100 Most Influential People" is a mixture of artists, scientists, politicians, and activists. While it's not about who is the nicest or most likable person in the world (Donald Trump has made the list six times), it is a serious honor, and the mark of a major player, to be included.

Zendaya made it onto TIME100 in 2022 at the age of just 25. TIME says it chooses people by considering "Who shaped the year? Who stood up? Who stood out?" Denis Villeneuve, director of Dune, was invited to write about why Zendaya deserves to be on the list: "[she] uses authenticity as a new superpower. She seems fearless, her roots run deep, and I love that she still laughs like a kid ... This is only the beginning."

We fell in love with Zendaya because she's so entertaining and relatable. But the making of a cultural icon is about more than just likability or beauty. Zendaya has made interesting work that people didn't love, but she found exciting. She's influential because she has integrity.

ICE CREAM

Zendaya's favorite food is ice cream. She can also bite straight into it without getting those zings in her teeth. "Usually people have sensitivity in their teeth, but I don't," she says. Her favorite ice cream is Jeni's Brown Butter Almond Brittle, which she says helped her get through filming intense scenes in *Euphoria*.

INSTAGRAM

With more than 150 million followers, Zendaya is currently the 24th most-followed person on Instagram. Her varied feed features fashion shoots and behind the scenes snaps, as well as the occasional Tom Holland-related update. For his birthday in June 2022, she posted a photo of them together with the caption: "Happiest of birthdays to the one who makes me the happiest."

I IS ALSO FOR...

ICONS

When it comes to style, Zendaya says her icons are music legends Diana Ross and Cher. In fact, she says Cher's wardrobe of Bob Mackie gowns is the celebrity closet she'd most like to rummage through. "Cher, if you ever want to style me, Law and I would love it."

J

IS FOR

JOAN OF ARC

The annual Met Gala is an opportunity to do more than wear a pretty dress on the red (or in this case, pink) carpet. Attendees must look their best while dressing according to the theme, carefully chosen by *Vogue* Editor-in-Chief Anna Wintour, who also vets the guest list and decides exactly which table everyone will sit at. (And yes, there is a bad table.)

In 2018, the theme was "Heavenly Bodies: Fashion and the Catholic Imagination". Zendaya channeled 15th-century Catholic martyr Joan of Arc, who was burned at the stake aged 19 for crimes of heresy, including witchcraft and dressing as a man.

Zendaya's Versace outfit was made of overlapping studded armor plates and lengths of sequinned chainmail, with a semi-transparent dress underneath to protect her from the sharp metal. She wore her hair short like Joan of Arc's, but opted for sky-high silver heels instead of military boots.

A slightly out-of-breath Zendaya told the red carpet interviewer the dress was "heavy... really heavy!"

J IS ALSO FOR...

JACOB ELORDI

Towering Australian actor Jacob Elordi plays Nate in *Euphoria*, a messed-up jock type with anger issues. Although they kept it private, Zendaya and Jacob were rumored to have dated for at least a year before splitting in 2020. They have continued to support each other publicly, with Jacob congratulating Zendaya on her Emmy win in September 2020. Good to see there are no hard feelings.

JOHN DAVID WASHINGTON

Actor John David Washington played Zendaya's boyfriend in the movie *Malcolm & Marie* (see page 65). Although he is the older of the two, John David said he looked up to Zendaya: "She has far more experience than I do in the industry. I've only been in it for seven years. She's been in it longer, so I'm learning from her."

JEWELRY

Zendaya owns a yellow diamond ring from fine jeweler Bulgari that she bought as a "splurge". Apparently she got the "employee discount"! She has been an ambassador for the brand since 2020 and starred in their 2022 campaign film alongside Anne Hathaway. It's not all diamonds though: she is often seen in pieces from her mom's handmade jewelry line Kizzmet.

K
IS FOR

K.C. UNDERCOVER

Disney sitcom *K.C. Undercover*, which ran for three seasons from 2015-18, is about teenage spy K.C. who works with her parents to bring down evil-doers. Facing the challenges of schoolwork, friendship, and international spying all at once, the comedy action sequences elevate it a little, however the main draw is not the premise but Zendaya herself.

Zendaya was a producer on the show, which gave her more control over the storylines and her character development. In fact, she made the writers change her character's name from Katy to K.C., saying, "The title is whack. That's gonna change. Do I look like a Katy to you?"

Despite being only 16, she had figured out that a lot of roles for women look the same. Making K.C. socially awkward and a bit of a geek was a stepping stone to another non-stereotypical female role, and it was while working on the show that Zendaya learned she had been cast as the similarly socially outcast MJ in *Spider-Man: Homecoming,* a role that would go on to define her career.

K IS ALSO FOR...

KAMIL MCFADDEN

Zendaya met Kamil when he played her brother Ernie on *K.C. Undercover* and counts him as a close friend to this day, saying, "Kamil is like my brother." The pair play video games together and can occasionally be seen jumping on an Instagram Live to shoot the breeze.

KARATE

Zendaya insisted her character in *K.C. Undercover* be a karate specialist rather than an artsy girl. "[K.C.] can't dance; she can't sing. She can't do that stuff. There are other things that a girl can be." Hopefully she picked up a few tips from her dad Kazembe, who is a black belt in karate.

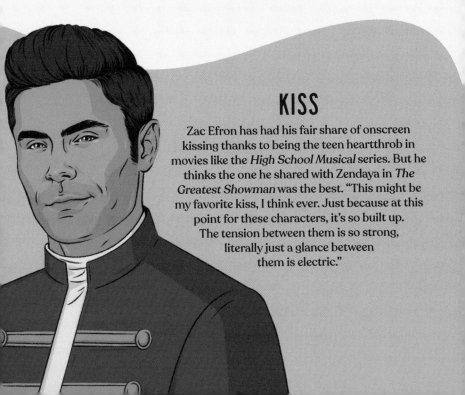

KISS

Zac Efron has had his fair share of onscreen kissing thanks to being the teen heartthrob in movies like the *High School Musical* series. But he thinks the one he shared with Zendaya in *The Greatest Showman* was the best. "This might be my favorite kiss, I think ever. Just because at this point for these characters, it's so built up. The tension between them is so strong, literally just a glance between them is electric."

KARAOKE

Zendaya likes to relax with her co-stars in the karaoke booth. As a talented singer, she's one of those people who actually sound good belting out their favorite song—her pick is "Crazy in Love" by her idol Beyoncé, confirmed by Timothée Chalamet who's joined her in the booth.

KNITTING

Zendaya's mom taught her the "old school hobby" of knitting. She says her skills are still basic: "All I can do is a scarf so... I can't give you a sweater or like a vest or anything." The craft helps Zendaya relax during long days on movie sets. "I like little tedious activities [that] keep your brain occupied."

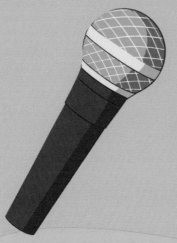

K IS ALSO FOR...

KINDNESS

Zendaya is often asked what she looks for in a partner. Along with respect, she says, "I would say kindness ... there's like this little spark they have, or this little special thing that they have, that just [makes] you feel safe and happy around them." She also advocates for being kind to yourself, and to "love who you are."

IS FOR

LIP SYNC BATTLE

Zendaya didn't need her real-life singing skills to face the ultimate performance challenge: lip-syncing for her life on Comedy Central's *Lip Sync Battle*. The show pits celebrities against each other as they deliver the most convincing and impressive miming performance to their choice of hit songs.

The level of commitment shown by the celebs varies: Academy Award winner Anne Hathaway made out with a rhinestone-encrusted mallet while impersonating Miley Cyrus for her version of "Wrecking Ball".

On the other hand, Pete Davidson of *Saturday Night Live* was clearly making up his unconvincing Justin Bieber performance as he went along. It was never in doubt that Zendaya would bring it, especially given who she was competing against... (See page 104 for more).

Lip-syncing to Bruno Mars' hit single "24k Magic", Zendaya choreographed a perfect routine. Walking onstage out of a private jet, and being surrounded by dancers and showgirls was sure to bring victory. After all, what could top that?

L IS ALSO FOR...
LOLA BUNNY

Zendaya voiced the character Lola Bunny in *Space Jam: A New Legacy* (2021). There was some tired internet backlash over the rabbit's appearance because the Zendaya version wore a basketball uniform that looked just like that of the male players, rather than the skimpier crop top and shorts Lola wore in the original 1990s movie.

LABRINTH

English singer and producer Labrinth composes the music for *Euphoria*, including the song "All For Us". Zendaya added her vocals to the song, and performed it in the Season One finale, when her character Rue's struggle with addiction is shown through a fully choreographed musical scene.

LOS ANGELES

Zendaya moved to Los Angeles with her family when she was cast in Disney Channel's *Shake it Up* in 2010 and has called it home ever since. Rather than living in busy central LA, Zendaya resides in a peaceful suburb north of the city. A self-described introvert, she loves to chill at home on her four-acre estate.

LAW ROACH

Zendaya calls her stylist Law "the most stylish person alive" and her "fashion soul mate." He started out running a vintage clothing store in his hometown of Chicago. Zendaya's dad introduced them after hearing about Law's talents through a mutual friend. Law and Z went on a shopping trip and have been working together ever since.

LOCS

For her Oscars red carpet look in 2015, Zendaya wore her hair in locs, also known as dreadlocks. After one TV anchor made a racist joke suggesting she smelt like weed, Zendaya spoke up about "ignorant slurs" based on racial stereotypes, calling the comment "outrageously offensive."

L IS ALSO FOR...

LEMONADE

For the song "All Night", from her masterpiece album *Lemonade* (2016), Beyoncé invited young stars including Zendaya and Halle and Chloe Bailey to appear in the video. Zendaya called the experience of posing with Beyoncé "one of the most beautiful things I've ever had the honor of being [a part] of."

MALCOLM & MARIE

Working as both producer and star, Zendaya collaborated with her *Euphoria* director Sam Levinson on the 2021 movie *Malcolm & Marie*.

Like millions of others in the summer of 2020, Zendaya was restless while staying at home during the Covid-19 lockdown. "I asked Sam if there was a world in which we could shoot something in my house or somewhere else. There was no intention other than to allow us to all be creative together, and to get our crew from *Euphoria* paid."

Zendaya put her own money into the production, which, due to Covid restrictions, could only have 12 people on set at a time and was filmed in just one location: a house in Carmel, the only county in California that allowed filming that summer.

The drama follows an argument between Zendaya's character Marie and her movie director boyfriend Malcolm (played by John David Washington). The movie is a testament to the cast and crew's love of creativity, made under the most difficult circumstances.

M IS ALSO FOR...

MOM

Zendaya's mom Claire Stoermer is a teacher with German heritage. Setting a hard-working example for her daughter, she stayed behind in Oakland to continue teaching while Zendaya moved to LA to start her career. Zendaya says, "Watching her [teach] was magical; it instilled within me a true appreciation of and devotion to the importance of education."

MOTTO

Zendaya is a deep well of wisdom. When asked by *Vanity* Fair magazine what her motto is, she simply replied "don't be an asshole." It sounds straightforward, but in reality, how many of us can recognize when we're the one being the asshole? There are so many stories about famous people believing their own hype and becoming intolerable. Maybe if Hollywood adopted Zendaya's motto, these sorts of people would avoid becoming their worst selves.

MULLET

The most cutting-edge look Zendaya has ever attempted was a mullet for the 2016 Grammys red carpet. The divisive style had a heavy blonde fringe at the front, with longer, darker strands at the back. "I got dragged for my mullet at the time, but kids love mullets now," Zendaya quipped in 2021.

MOULIN ROUGE

Zendaya's favorite classic movie is *Moulin Rouge*, a 2001 musical about an ill-fated love affair between a Parisian showgirl (Nicole Kidman) and a hopeless romantic (Ewan McGregor). She says, "Moulin Rouge is prob one of my all time favorite movies... I used to watch it over and over." The director Baz Luhrmann also made *Romeo + Juliet*, which is heavily referenced in *Euphoria*, including the scene where Rue and Jules kiss in the swimming pool.

MIDNIGHT

Before Noon, there was Midnight, Zendaya's beloved childhood dog, a black schnauzer. When he passed away in 2015, she wrote a public note on Instagram thanking him "for being one of the most loyal men in my life, for loving me unconditionally and for cuddling me whenever I needed."

M IS ALSO FOR...

MUSIC INDUSTRY

For a long time, it was a mystery as to why Zendaya's second album was never released. Recently, she has opened up about the unique pressures of working in music, from greater invasions of privacy to being ripped off by legal contracts: "If anyone asks my number one advice, for [the entertainment] industry in general but mostly the music industry, it's look over those contracts, every single word, and don't sign anything that isn't worth it to you. You are worth more than they will say that you are."

IS FOR

NOON

Zendaya has had several dogs, but one pup has really laid its claim on her heart. Noon, a miniature schnauzer, has lived with Zendaya since 2015, after her previous dog Midnight passed away. Zendaya excitedly posted on Instagram: "Most of you know I lost my baby Midnight a while ago, and I thought I could never love another pet again... until this little angel was given to me on Christmas Eve."

As well as being cute, Noon has a naughty side: Zendaya says his Hogwarts house would be Slytherin and out of all the Harry Potter characters he's most like Professor Snape because "he'll be cold to you, but he'll look out for you."

Whatever his flaws, Zendaya adores him, describing the dog as her "best friend" and "beloved son" and often taking him with her to set for extra love and support.

And Noon no longer needs his owner to post about him because he has his own account, @nooncolemann, where he has over 27,000 followers.

NEGATIVITY

When asked in her *Vogue* "73 Questions" interview how she deals with negativity, Zendaya said serenely, "I try to keep in mind that everyone is dealing with something that we have no idea about." But when she saw someone fat shaming a girl online, she pulled no punches, tweeting, "this is stupid … she is fine as hell head to toe and guaranteed doesn't know you exist my man. As for her, slay on queen."

NAME

Let's settle this once and for all, for everyone hopelessly searching online for the answer to "Is it Zendaya or Zendaya?" It's Zen-day-a, not Zen-dye-a. The "day" is pronounced like "SaturDAY". Zen-DAY-a. The name Zendaya is based on a Shona name that means "to give thanks," with an extra "zen" twist from Zendaya's dad.

N IS ALSO FOR...

NO WAY HOME

The third in Zendaya's string of Spider-Man movies gives us a lot of fun MJ and Ned moments as they help Spidey deal with parallel universe drama. The love interest in a Spider-Man movie is always in danger of falling off a tall building, and MJ's time finally came. It was Andrew Garfield's character who saved her, providing a moment of redemption for him after he was unable to save his own parallel universe MJ.

IS FOR

THE OA

The OA was a mind-bending TV show following Prairie, a woman who wakes up with amnesia and is desperate to figure out what happened. Zendaya appeared in the critically-acclaimed second season, playing Fola, a dedicated puzzle-solver who is determined to discover the secrets of a strange house that could unlock the mystery of Prairie's disappearance.

Fola introduces private detective Karim to an online game called "Q Symphony", making cryptic statements such as, "It's not a game, it's a puzzle." (Turns out—spoiler alert—it's actually a portal to another dimension invented by an evil tech guy). Karim later rescues Fola from the house, mysteriously aged and close to death. Will she recover, return to the house and discover its secrets? Sadly not, because the show was canceled after its second season, leaving many clues without answers.

Zendaya said she liked *The OA* before she was cast, so she may have hustled herself a cameo just for fun. Maybe one day it will return and Fola will get her closure.

O IS ALSO FOR...

OAKLAND

Zendaya was born and raised in Oakland, California. She is very proud of her hometown, the most diverse city in the US, and has said, "Oakland is such a cultural melting pot and it has so much history, especially when it comes to civil rights." In the 1960s, Oakland was the birthplace of far-left political group the Black Panther Party, who campaigned for black nationalism and protested against police brutality, and still has many community organizations working for change.

OSCARS RED CARPET

You can rely on Zendaya to dress unpredictably, so she's become a highly-anticipated presence on the biggest red carpet of them all: the Oscars. Her looks so far include: a white satin Vivienne Westwood dress (2015); a billowing one-shoulder Giambattista Valli Couture dress in chocolate brown, an unusual color for the red carpet (2018); a neon-yellow cut-out custom Valentino gown inspired by Cher (2021); and another Valentino number—a sequinned maxi skirt with ultra-cropped white shirt (2022). We are still waiting for her Oscar nomination for Best Actress...

ON TOUR

Early fans of Zendaya got the chance to see her live on stage during her pop star era. From August 2012 to November 2014, she played arenas and amphitheaters across the US as part of her Swag It Out Tour. For her show at the Art & Soul Festival in Oakland, the title song was introduced by a high school marching band, six years before Beyoncé would use a marching band in her legendary Coachella performance.

P

IS FOR

POP STAR

Zendaya is a triple threat. She has the dance skills needed to master routines, and while you don't necessarily *have* to be an amazing singer to be a captivating pop star, she has proved her vocal abilities by singing a cappella on social media. As an actor, she can also deliver engaging performances onstage and in music videos.

The debut album *Zendaya* had a promising first hit with "Replay", which reached number 40 on the Billboard Hot 100–if that doesn't sound high, bear in mind Taylor Swift's first single peaked in the same position. But then things went quiet. It seems like acting is a better fit for the level of personal privacy Zendaya wants to maintain. "I don't know if I could ever be a pop star. It's because as an actor, there's a level of anonymity that I get to have," she says. Zendaya continues to channel her musical side by contributing to the soundtracks of her acting projects, and tweeted in spring 2022: "I still really love it, so the kindness and support I've received ... just for a little tiny toe dip back into some music means the absolute world to me."

P IS ALSO FOR...

PAINTING

When she's not busy working, Zendaya tries to take her mind off things by painting in a journal. Her friend and *Euphoria* co-star Hunter Schafer gave her the journal, into which she daubs watercolors. Zendaya says the aim of her hobby "is to try not to be so damn controlling all the time and just paint."

PHOTOGRAPHY

Zendaya collects cameras, including the analog old-fashioned kind that takes film, such as her trendy Contax T2 and Contax G2, and Polaroid cameras. She asks for advice from the photographers and cinematographers she works with. Talking about Marcell Rév who works on *Euphoria*, she said, "when I'm on set, I'll ask him what all the names of the different lights are and what they do and why they need them." She has even hinted, "Maybe I'll become a director, or a director of photography."

PRINCESS TIANA

From *Cinderella* to *Alice in Wonderland*, Disney is in the middle of a huge project to make live-action versions of their beloved animated movies. Zendaya was rumored to be in the running to play Ariel in *The Little Mermaid*, although the role eventually went to Halle Bailey. But she says her favorite princess is Tiana from *The Princess and the Frog* "because she has an attitude." Nothing has yet been announced for this movie, so there is still hope!

PROJECT RUNWAY

The guest judge on the Season 15 finale of *Project Runway* (2016) was, in the words of supermodel presenter Heidi Klum, the "beautiful Zendaya". She helped the other judges—Heidi, fashion journalist Nina Garcia, and designer Zac Posen—to pick between four finalists. They eventually crowned Erin and, unlike the other judges, Zendaya said she would actually wear her showstopper: a banana-print jacket.

PRIVACY

After photos emerged in the tabloid press of her kissing Tom Holland, Zendaya said, "when you really love and care about somebody, some moments or things, you wish were your own." Tom, for his part, added, "One of the downsides of our fame is that privacy isn't really in our control anymore, and a moment that you think is between two people that love each other very much is now a moment that is shared with the entire world." Meanwhile, Zendaya has praised her fans for being "really respectful of my boundaries and the things that I choose to keep a little bit more private."

P IS ALSO FOR...

PET PEEVES & PREFERENCES

Quick fire round:

- Zendaya's pet peeve is chipped nail polish ("It's either all on, or all off. You'll never catch me slipping.")

- She prefers her pancakes without syrup; butter or Nutella will do

- She doesn't like coffee or fizzy drinks

- Showers over baths

- Binge-watching over weekly episodes

- No orange-flavored food

Q
IS FOR

QUOTES

"I promote self-love and I think I have to live that too. So, I definitely try not to be critical of myself and my appearance."

– as told to *Essence*, 2020

"A lot of what I do, specifically within fashion, is a tribute to the fashion icons who came before me—many of whom are Black women."

– as told to *Essence*, 2020

"I have that pride in knowing that I'm an African American. I think when you develop pride in where you're from, then you have more respect and understanding in terms of where other people are from also."

– as told to *Hunger* magazine, 2015

"Everybody has an opinion. Everybody has a way that they see that your career should go, and sometimes you just got to stick with your gut and stick with your instincts and stick with your personal vision ... If you're trying to be something that you are not, will people will realize at some point that you're not being authentic."

– as told to *Hunger* magazine, 2015

"I think my fans pretty much understand me. They know I don't leave my house, they know that I'm lazy, they know that I'm pretty open but also pretty private. I think we have, in a weird way, a pretty close relationship. My fans get me for sure."

– as told to *Allure,* 2019

"There's literally injustice happening every second. It's intense and it's overwhelming, and I think a lot of young people are feeling that. But what do we do about it? All I can say is try to find a balance between doing the work and still not letting it destroy you as a person and destroy your hope and faith in humanity."

– as told to *Allure,* 2019

"It's important to raise your voice in things you feel passionate about, and things that you know about. Don't raise your voice just to raise your voice, if you have nothing behind it and don't know what you're talking about. But if you take the time to learn about something, and educate yourself, then you have a voice, and you're allowed to use it."

– as told to *Hunger* magazine, 2015

"I love getting glammed, don't get me wrong. I love the hair and makeup and fashion and that's my stuff, but like nine times out of ten I'm not doing that every day, I'm just chilling."

– as told to BBC Radio 1, 2018

RONNIE SPECTOR

It always seemed likely that Zendaya would use her singing and acting talents to portray one of history's powerhouse musicians. In a potentially Oscar-worthy role, she will be playing rock'n'roll singer Ronnie Spector in the upcoming biopic.

Co-founder and fronting singer of the iconic 1960s girl group, The Ronettes, Ronnie's voluminous hair, sweet voice and confidence made her the group's most recognizable member. She married the famous music producer Phil Spector, but he tried to stop her going on tour or recording music. After splitting from him, Ronnie got the group back together and fought for her right to own her own music.

After Ronnie's death in January 2022, Zendaya posted on Instagram: "Thank you for sharing your life with me, I could listen to your stories for hours and hours ... I hope to make you proud."

Ronnie herself chose Zendaya to portray her onscreen, and Z will also be one of the movie's producers.

R IS ALSO FOR...

RUE

Zendaya has been widely praised for her portrayal of Rue in *Euphoria*. Rue is the character who mostly closely represents the show's creator Sam Levinson (see page 97), who has also struggled with drug addiction. The oversized burgundy hoodie that Zendaya wears to play Rue was auctioned off for $8,000 in 2020, with profits going to healthcare workers.

REWRITE THE STARS

Although there are bigger, flashier tunes in *The Greatest Showman*, the sweet romantic ballad sung by Zendaya and Zac Efron is one of the best. This is the number in which they first address their feelings and outline the apparently impossible obstacles facing them. It is played later when the two characters realize that they can in fact write their own future together.

REPLAY

A slinky R'n'B-influenced song about obsessive love, "Replay" was the first single from the album *Zendaya*. The beat came first, created by producer Mick Schultz, then Zendaya and lyricists Tiffany Fred and Phamous came in to craft the song. Schultz says, "When Zendaya [first] heard it, she came to my studio to record it and the song came out pretty quickly after that. She's incredible and a superstar!". The song is still Zendaya's biggest hit, going platinum in the US.

IS
FOR

SPIDER-MAN

The Spider-Man trilogy brought Zendaya into the Marvel cinematic universe and launched her career as a Hollywood megastar. It was also a special time for her personally. In her own words, "When I did the first movie, I was 19. It's pretty special to have grown up all together and be a part of [a] legacy."

We've seen MJ transform from a side character to having a central role; making friends, falling in love with a superhero, helping to save the world, and (most importantly, kids!) maintaining her grades in the process. She's a refreshing heroine with a personality and a backbone, with a cute-but-grungy look that shows us what she cares about—watch out for her "VOTES FOR WOMEN" t-shirt and ones with images of the poet Sylvia Plath and the historical figure Joan of Arc (for more on that, see page 49).

The end of No Way Home left Peter and MJ worse off than where they started. He's still in love with her, but she has no idea who she is. Luckily, there are plenty more movies in the works.

S IS ALSO FOR...

SMALLFOOT

2018 animated movie *Smallfoot* is about yetis who are trying to prove humans ("smallfeet") exist, with Zendaya providing the voice for the character of Meechee. The movie's main legacy is the internet meme "Zendaya is Meechee", a reference to actor and content creator Gabriel Gundacker's viral spoof song, in which he sings the nonsensical string of words on the movie's promo poster.

SELENA GOMEZ

A young Zendaya can be seen dancing in a 2009 commercial for Sears. Zendaya, dressed in a heavily-accessorized red-and-black outfit with a tiered skirt, is one of a group of kid dancers giving it 100 percent behind the main star Selena Gomez. The soundtrack to the elaborate advert is an original Fallout Boy-style song called "I'm Gonna Arrive".

SHAKE IT UP

Zendaya's big break came when she got the role of Rocky Blue, starring alongside Bella Thorne in the Disney Channel show *Shake It Up*. The show's premiere was watched by approximately 6.2 million viewers, making it a huge success. It ran to three seasons, with 75 episodes and three soundtrack albums recorded along the way.

STOMP OUT BULLYING

Zendaya and her Spider-Man co-stars filmed a video for the Stomp Out Bullying campaign in 2017. Zendaya said that bullies "[don't] understand the power of inclusion, diversity, and kindness". She's previously advised victims to "realize that you're not alone... you have people to talk to whether it be a teacher, mentor, [or] parent."

SILKWORM

Zendaya's very first audition was for her school play: a production of Roald Dahl's *James and the Giant Peach*. She was given the non-speaking part of the Silkworm. Zendaya reviews her own performance highly: "I was killing it, I was reacting and giving face and being the best dang silkworm there was."

S IS ALSO FOR...

SAM LEVINSON

Sam Levinson is a writer and director who's worked with Zendaya on several projects. He created *Euphoria* and also wrote and directed the movie *Malcolm & Marie*. Sam says, "what I love the most about Z is she's able to go to those dark places and then as soon as I call 'cut', she's hanging out behind the monitor, eating Cheesecake Factory and cracking jokes ... She's one of the most grounded human beings I know."

TOM HOLLAND

Zendaya and Tom met during her audition for *Spider-Man: Homecoming*, a situation where casting directors are looking for chemistry between actors. It turns out they did have chemistry; Zendaya was cast as MJ, and they have been working together ever since. They have racked up three movies together and one lip-sync battle for the ages. They've also popped up on each other's Instagram profiles over the years, with Tom Holland posting various messages in which he light-heartedly calls Zendaya "mate." In 2018, he posted her Met Gala outfit with the caption: "All hail the queen. Killing it mate." Sounds more like boyfriend behavior than mate behavior, but okay!

At some point, their adorable friendship turned into something more. The press published photos of the two kissing in Tom's car in July 2021. They've cheerfully brushed off comments about their height difference (Tom: "she's not *that* much taller!") and, while they've been spotted together a lot, they're keeping their private life together totally private—for now.

T IS ALSO FOR...

TIMBALAND

Zendaya worked with legendary producer Timbaland on at least two songs, including the ethereal "Close Up". They crafted a slinky R'n'B sound for Zendaya's second album, but sadly the record was never released. Timbaland, who has worked with Beyoncé and Missy Elliot, was excited to collaborate with Zendaya, and publicly supported her during Locsgate (see page 62), tweeting "Preach !!!!!!!"

TIMOTHÉE CHALAMET

Zendaya's *Dune* co-star Timothée Chalamet seems to have chemistry with just about everyone, so it's no surprise they hit it off. Zendaya said it was obvious immediately: "Oh, this is great, we're gonna be besties, I can tell." They've been spotted getting dinner together: a true sign that the friendship is real.

TRAPEZE SKILLS

Zendaya trained to do her own trapeze swings and catches in *The Greatest Showman*, as the director Michael Gracey wanted "to use the stunt doubles as little as possible." After overcoming her fear during training, Zendaya arrived on set to find "the rig was like 15 to 20 feet taller, and there was no net." Ever a pro, she filmed the stunts anyway, prompting Hugh Jackman to call her a "badass."

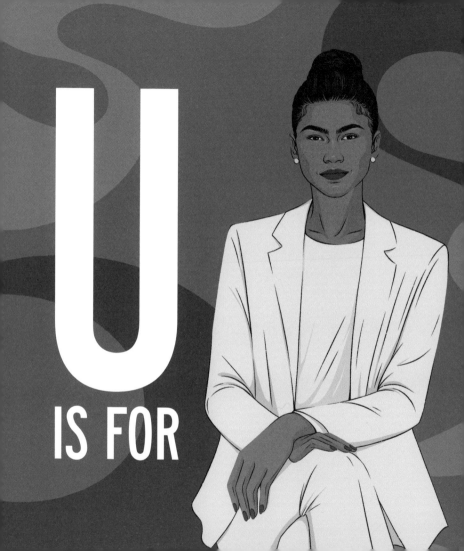

U

IS FOR

UN AMBASSADOR

The United Nations appoints youth ambassadors to represent some of its most important projects for children and young people, and in 2014 Zendaya got the call. She was the spokesperson for that year's UNICEF Halloween charity drive, where trick-or-treating kids collect money for charity as well as candy for themselves.

Zendaya said, "I started doing this in school and I think what's really important is it got me in the spirit of learning how to give back at a young age."

In 2015, Zendaya stepped up to an even more important role as an ambassador for UNAIDS, the program to tackle HIV and AIDS. She traveled to South Africa and met young leaders who "had amazing ideas on how they could fix it … it made me want to step up my game."

Zendaya spoke out about removing the stigma around HIV testing: "[It's] really important that as young people, we're not afraid to have the discussion … so nobody will be ashamed to go get tested."

U IS ALSO FOR...

UMBRELLA

Riding high after her 10/10 performance of Bruno Mars' "24k Magic" on Comedy Central's *Lip Sync Battle* (see page 59), Zendaya thought she had her 2017 battle against Tom Holland firmly in the bag. Unfortunately for her, he was about to deliver a 100/10 version of "Singin' in the Rain" mashed up with "Umbrella", which would define his career and become beloved to all who watched it. Tom says, "I get more compliments from dancing in the rain in fishnets than I do for anything [else] I've done." Sore loser Zendaya says, "I'm still feeling the effects," but admits, "He obviously killed it." The clip has been viewed almost 140 million times on YouTube.

UNREALISTIC BEAUTY STANDARDS

One thing Zendaya will not do is make other women feel bad about themselves. In 2015, the magazine *Modeliste* published photos that had been retouched to make her look thinner. Hitting back at the unnecessary editing, she posted that she was "shocked when I found my 19-year-old hips and torso quite manipulated. These are the things that make women self conscious, that create the unrealistic ideals of beauty that we have." She also posted the original version of the picture to show that she is perfect the way she is, adding, "Anyone who knows who I am knows I stand for honest and pure self love."

UMMMMMMM

Zendaya says her most overused word is "um". In fact, despite always finding something smart to say when being asked the same questions over and over again on press tours, she is convinced she says "'um' far too much. I watch my interviews and I'm like, you sound dumb." We are going to have to disagree with (the very articulate) Zendaya on this one.

VEGETARIAN

Zendaya has been a vegetarian since she was 11 years old. She says, "My main reason for being a vegetarian is that I'm an animal lover—definitely not because I love vegetables." For her, the moment of realization came when she was on a road trip with her dad and they drove past a slaughterhouse. She asked him what was going on in there, and he explained. It was an eye-opening moment that helped her connect the meat she ate (she especially loved her mom's turkey burgers) with the animals it came from. She says, "I think when you're younger you don't really realize where meat comes from, right? ... But then you grow up and you realize what happens and how you get the meat, and I was just not down for it."

Zendaya says she doesn't miss eating meat at all, although it's not always easy to completely eliminate it. She was stressed out when she discovered her favorite food, chicken-flavored noodles, actually do have chicken in them: "I felt horrible that I didn't know that. I don't know, I guess I just thought it was like artificial flavoring, but I guess there is real chicken in it."

VERSACE ON THE FLOOR

As well as dressing up as Bruno Mars for her lip-sync battle, Zendaya appeared in the video for his song "Versace on the Floor". Bruno personally called Zendaya to ask her to play his love interest in what is half-music video, half-ode to the fashion house Versace. Bruno plays the piano in one hotel room while Zendaya sits on the bed next door. In the final seconds of the video, we see that the Versace dress is, finally, on the floor.

VILLAIN

Zendaya's roles so far have been pretty lovable for the most part, but she has a dark side she wants to unleash: "I've always wanted to play a heightened, more theatrical kind of villain." Actress Vivica A. Fox has publicly rooted for her to be cast as her daughter in *Kill Bill 3*, which will definitely involve women in catsuits being theatrically villainous. Zendaya hedged, "I'm very flattered that she would think of me. But, you know, it's just an idea."

V IS ALSO FOR...

VIRGO

Whether you believe in star signs or not, thinking about them can help people identify their personal character traits. Virgos (born between 23 August and 22 September) are usually described as practical and grounded, but also a little strict. Zendaya admits, "I'm a Virgo, I'm a perfectionist. It's hard to let things go and I've not been easy on myself sometimes."

W IS FOR

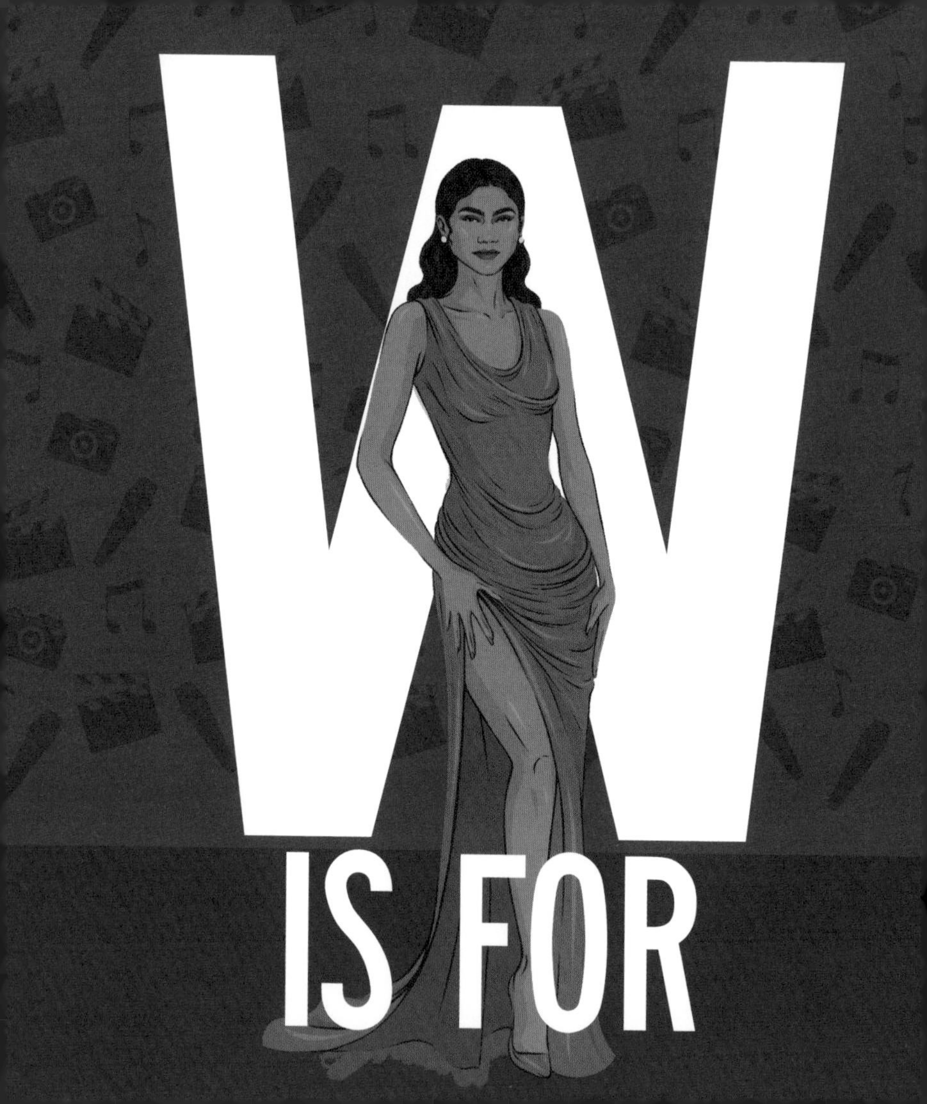

WORKAHOLIC

Zendaya has two modes: chilling at home, and working with a ferocious intensity. Rather than struggling with motivation, she's perhaps a little addicted to her work. Like other workaholics, she finds purpose and happiness in being productive and busy.

One problem workaholics often have is that they feel worried about "not doing enough" if they're not constantly working towards a goal. Zendaya explains: "I hate spare time. I just don't know what I'm doing when I'm not working."

So what does a workaholic do when there's no work to do? During the Covid-19 pandemic, Zendaya stopped working for the first time since age 14. She says it was "a very scary thing to confront and work through, because I don't really know Zendaya outside of the Zendaya who works. I didn't realize how much my job and my art were a part of my identity as a human." While she's probably never going to stop pushing herself, Zendaya has made herself a promise to take time to "just be happy, and just be alive for a second."

WOMEN'S MARCH

The Women's March on Washington in 2017 was a huge protest for gender equality and civil rights. Zendaya marched in solidarity with approximately 500,000 others in Washington and millions more across the US and the world. She wore a sweatshirt that read "Respect / Protect / Love The Black Woman" and tweeted that she "couldn't be more proud" of the attendees.

WILD 'N OUT

Zendaya featured on an episode of zany improv show *Wild 'n Out* in 2015. Zendaya and host Nick Cannon went head-to-head to avoid spitting out a mouthful of water while the other cast members tried to make them laugh. A cringe moment ensued when comedian Matt Rife grabbed her face and asked for her number, prompting chaos in the studio as other cast members told him to back off, yelling "she's too young." A stony-faced Zendaya wagged her finger at Rife to signify "no" (and of course she went on to win the challenge).

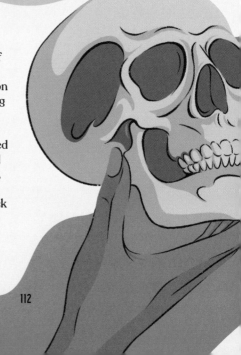

W IS ALSO FOR...

WILLIAM SHAKESPEARE

Acting in Shakespeare's plays is the best training an actor can get. When she was growing up, Zendaya's mom was the house manager at the California Shakespeare Theater. The young Zendaya began by helping backstage before acting in plays like *As You Like It*. She says her favorite Shakespeare heroine is Viola from *Twelfth Night* and her favorite line is: "If music be the food of love, play on."

X IS FOR

ZENDAYA X...

Zendaya has gone beyond modeling to make meaningful collaborations with fashion houses, working on projects where she gets lots of creative input. Lending her name to these collabs and being part of the design and marketing process makes her more of an equal partner in an industry where young women are often at risk of exploitation.

Speaking at a *Vogue* conference, Zendaya said that when embarking on projects, you should "make sure that you've learned as much as you can about the business portion so that you can really run things and create things on your own and [avoid] that situation where you wake up one day, and you're like 'oh, I've been working so hard but I don't have anything to show for it.'"

The high fashion brands she works with value Zendaya for her insight: "I know my fans, and I know what's important to them."

Having a say means she can insist on size inclusivity. "I'm not going to make clothes my sister or my niece or any of the women in my family can't wear," she says.

X IS ALSO FOR...
X VALENTINO

Zendaya was the face and creative partner of historic French fashion house Valentino for its 2022 collection Rendez-Vous, featuring the brand's signature deep pink color. This partnership has been thriving for years: Valentino made Zendaya's zingy yellow 2021 Oscars gown. Creative director Pierpaolo Piccioli heaped praise on his muse and collaborator, saying, "I chose Zendaya as a person, for what she stands for, and not as a model."

X TOMMY HILFIGER

Zendaya's 2019 Tommy Hilfiger collection was celebrated with a runway show at Paris fashion week. The show was inspired by the iconic Battle of Versailles in 1973, a fashion show where French designers competed against American ones to present the best designs. The Americans won the original Battle, but this show had only winners: the presentation was graced by a diverse array of Black models hand-picked by Zendaya, including Pat Cleveland, who had modeled in the 1973 show at a time when it was still very unusual to see people of color on the catwalk.

"X" WITH PRINCE ROYCE

In 2017, Zendaya sang in English and Spanish on the track "X", a collaboration with singer Prince Royce about reconnecting with an ex. The song is a chill fusion of bachata (a style of music from the Dominican Republic) and smooth R'n'B vocals—it would be perfect on a relaxed Sunday playlist. Zendaya did a great job conveying the emotion of the song despite not actually speaking Spanish. "I have no idea what I'm saying!" she joked.

Y IS FOR

YOUTUBE

Every young, glamorous Hollywood star has a secret from their past: their first YouTube video. The 20-year-old Zendaya filmed her reaction to watching her first clip and physically cringed at her (adorable) 14-year-old self declaring her channel was "a place for happy smiley faces and lots of love and dancing."

Adult Zendaya described it as "the most annoying thing I've ever seen," explaining that it was a shiny, inoffensive persona she felt she had to perform for her Disney Channel fans.

Zendaya later moved from YouTube to her own app ("Zendaya: The App"), full of short videos that gave cute insights into her life. "I wanted a place where I could make my own content and really be in control of what I create," she said.

Her videos became more relatable, like a tour through her current Netflix watch list. She laughs about her early YouTube efforts to please an imaginary audience online, saying, "I swear I've always been like I am now," meaning the grounded version of Zendaya we know and love.

YOUNGEST SIBLING

Zendaya is the youngest in her family and has five older brothers and sisters: Austin, Katianna, Annabella, Julien, and Kaylee. They are her dad's kids from a previous marriage and are quite a bit older— in fact, Zendaya was "born an auntie" and has several nieces and nephews who are older as well as younger than her. The family are close, and Zendaya calls her siblings her "heroes."

YARA SHAHIDI

Zendaya's close friend Yara Shahidi says that "Zendaya is like a big sister to me." They both started acting at a young age and are passionate about social justice. Yara wrote in *Glamour* magazine: "There's a misconception in this industry that everybody who looks like you, or may, at first, seem like you, must be your competition. What I so deeply respect about Zendaya is that she's actively helping to dismantle that myth." Yara and Zendaya have performed together twice, when Zendaya guest starred on Yara's show *Black-ish* and also as voice actors on the animated movie *Smallfoot*.

Y IS ALSO FOR...

YOUNGEST PRODUCER

In 2022, Zendaya was nominated for an Emmy for her work as a producer on *Euphoria*. This is amazing in itself, but doubly so because she is in fact the youngest person ever nominated for an Emmy as a producer. Emmys are voted for by Zendaya's peers in the industry, so it means her work is both popular and respected. She was also nominated for best actress in a drama and for two songs on the soundtrack, "Elliot's Song" and "I'm Tired".

ZEN-DAYA

Zendaya's dad Kazembe chose her name partly because he has "a thing for Zs and zen, very nice and calm". Zendaya lives up to this, describing herself as chilled-out. While she is forthright when she sees injustice, Zendaya happily calls herself "Zen-daya" and says her emotions usually don't get too intense: "I never get too excited, I never get too mad, never get too happy, never get too anything."

Zendaya is calm in real life but lets out all her emotions at work. Playing a character who gets into a big fight with her boyfriend in *Malcolm & Marie* was cathartic: "I'm not a very argumentative person, but it's nice to just ... get sh*t out that maybe I had pent up or hadn't said."

Part of "being zen" is trying not to worry about the things you can't change. Zendaya's character MJ in the Spider-Man movies embodies this attitude, hinting that she may have had input into how MJ was written. Her line, "If you expect disappointment, then you can never really be disappointed," is a funny twist on the philosophy of accepting what life throws at you.

Z IS ALSO FOR...

ZZZZZ

Zendaya is a busy bee, so she needs a lot of rest to balance out the hard work. She struggles with mornings (like the rest of us), and says, "I am usually one to sleep in ... I'm definitely a lie-around type. I'll debate for a good few minutes whether I want to get up or try to sleep for another 10 minutes." Given how busy she is and how much she travels, Zendaya often has to seize the chance to sleep in odd places: "I can sleep anywhere ... I love sleeping." Zzzzzzzzz.

ZAC EFRON

Zac and Zendaya were thrown in at the deep end on the set of *The Greatest Showman*. "We had a brief introduction and the next thing you know we were hauled up into the air," recalls Zac. Working together on the movie's intense trapeze stunts was "a good bonding experience" for the pair, and Zac came out of the experience with a high regard for Zendaya, who he calls "an epic person to work with."

ZENDAYA–THE ALBUM

Obviously, Z stands for Zendaya, but it also stands for *Zendaya*. The album, which came out in 2013, has 12 tracks, including the lead single "Replay", which she helped to write. One of Zendaya's favorite songs on the album was "Fireflies", a dance track about putting your hands up in the air, which sounds like a slinky Chloe x Halle track mixed with "We Found Love" by Calvin Harris and Rihanna.

AUTHOR SATU HÄMEENAHO-FOX

Satu is a writer and editor from London. A pop culture fan and theorist, she has written books on celebrities, fashion history, and nature. You can find her either in a museum gift shop or tending to her orchard.

ILLUSTRATOR SARAH MADDEN

Sarah is a UK based designer and illustrator with a passion for projects that aim to bring a little joy to the everyday. Sarah's personal work is reflective, focusing on themes of personal wellbeing. You can see more of her work at **sarahmadden.co.uk**

QUOTES

5: "Here Comes A Superstar... Zendaya", *New You* (newyou.com). **8:** "Zendaya Replies to Fans on the Internet", *GQ* (youtube.com). **9:** "Zendaya Gets Stitches After Kitchen Injury...", *People* (people.com). **11:** "Zendaya at the Women's March on Washington", *Zendaya* (youtube.com). **19:** "Zendaya: 'I'm Hollywood's acceptable version of a black girl'", *BBC News* (bbc.co.uk). **21:** "Denis Villeneuve on Zendaya's Role in 'Dune: Part 2'...", *Variety* (variety.com). **22:** "Father of Disney's Zendaya on Grooming a Young Star", *Wall Street Journal* (youtube.com). **24:** "Zendaya got her car stuck/snapchat story" (youtube.com); twitter.com/zendaya/status/1004237010247213056. **27:** "Euphoria review – so explicit it makes Skins look positively Victorian", *The Guardian* (theguardian.com). **28:** "Zendaya Replies to Fans on the Internet", *GQ* (youtube.com). **29:** "Zendaya's Top Five Makeup Tips", *Teen Vogue* (youtube.com). **31:** "Welcome to Zollywood", *GQ* (gq.com); "Zendaya Got Disney to Agree to a Feminist List of Demands for Her Show", *Self* (self.com); "Zendaya: Women Need Each Other's Voices Now More Than Ever", *Elle* (elle.com); "Zendaya Embraces That "True Feminism" Must Include Trans Women In The Narrative", *Seventeen* (seventeen.com). **42:** twitter.com/zendaya/status/233016311599493120. **43:** "#StayHome and Learn the Hula Dance with Zendaya", *Radio Disney* (youtube.com); "A complete timeline of 'Euphoria' costars Zendaya and Hunter Schafer's friendship", *Insider* (insider.com). **45:** "The 100 Most Influential People of 2022: Zendaya", *TIME* (time.com). **46:** "Zendaya Eats Ice Cream With Her Teeth", *Vanity Fair* (youtube.com). **47:** "9 Distinct Times Zendaya Paid Tribute to Style Icons and Pop Culture on the Red Carpet", *Pop Sugar* (popsugar.co.uk). **49:** "Zendaya, Nicki Minaj on vouge interview @ metgala 7 May 2018", Butter fish :3 (youtube.com). **51:** "John David Washington on Zendaya's Versatility...", *Variety* (variety.com). **53:** "That Time Zendaya Ruled In A Room Full Of Disney Execs...", *Huffpost* (huffingtonpost.co.uk). **55:** "Zendaya Got Disney to Agree to a Feminist List of Demands for Her Show", *Self* (self.com); "Zac Efron Admits His On-Screen Kiss with Zendaya in 'The Greatest Showman' Was His 'Favorite'", *People* (people.com). **56:** "Graham Norton Show || Zendaya likes to knit || Season 29 ep 10", Treshana Mcgrey (youtube.com). **57:** "Zendaya Applauded for the Way She Handled Gendered Question", *Complex* (complex.com). **62:** "Ariana Grande's Stylist Is Not Just Waiting in the Wings", *The New York Times* (nytimes.com); "Giuliana's Racist Comments about Zendaya's locs...", Haute Whispers (youtube.com); "Zendaya Says Giuliana Rancic's Infamous Comment...", *Vanity Fair* (vanityfair.com). **63:** "Zendaya on Cameo in Beyoncé's Lemonade...", *Essence* (essence.com). **65:** ""I Was So Desperate to Work": John David Washington on Making 'Malcolm & Marie' Amid the Pandemic", *The Hollywood Reporter* (hollywoodreporter.com). **66:** "Zendaya and Michelle Obama Deliver a VERY Important Message About Worldwide Education for Girls", *Teen Vogue* (teenvogue.com). **67:** "Zendaya Answers Personality Revealing Questions", Vanity Fair (youtube.com); "Zendaya Doesn't Regret her David Bowie Mullet", *W* (wmagazine.com). **68:** twitter.com/zendayastatus/434551375671066624. **69:** "Seeing Red: Zendaya to the Extreme", *Paper* (papermag.com). **71:** "Zendaya and Tom Holland Sort Their Dogs Into Hogwarts Houses", *Woof Republic* (woofrepublic.com). **76:** "Zendaya on How Oakland Molded Her", SWAY'S UNIVERSE (youtube.com). **79:** "Zendaya Doesn't Know If She 'Could Ever Be a Pop Star'...", *People* (people.com); twitter.com/zendaya/status/1499872622145769473. **80:** "Welcome to Zollywood", *GQ* (gq.com). **81:** "Zendaya Tells Colman Domingo How She Found New Purpose", *Interview* (interviewmagazine.com); "A Work of Art", *Essence* (essence.com); "18 Things You Need to Know About Zendaya", *Buzzfeed* (buzzfeed.com). **82:** "Tom Holland is in the Center of the Web", *GQ* (gq.com); "Zendaya on the cover of Vogue Italia...", *Vogue* (vogue.it). **83:** "Zendaya Shares 19 Facts About Herself", Glamour (youtube.com). **85:** "A Work of Art", *Essence* (essence.com); "Zendaya | Hunger Magazine Interview", Zen | Day (youtube.com). **86:** "Zendaya | Hunger Magazine Interview", Zen | Day (youtube.com); "How Zendaya Balances Her Public Persona and Personal Identity", *Allure* (allure.com). **87:** "Zendaya | Hunger Magazine Interview", Zen | Day (youtube.com); "You look a lot like... Zendaya on what fans say to her in the street", BBC Radio 1 (youtube.com). **91:** "Replay by Zendaya", Who Sampled (whosampled.com). **93:** "Here's Why Zendaya Says She's So "Grateful" For Her Spider-Man Experience", *E! News* (eonline.com). **96:** "SPIDER-MAN: HOMECOMING - Stomp Out Bullying PSA", Sony Pictures Entertainment (youtube.com); "Zendaya Wishes She Had Michael Jackson's Dance Moves", W Magazine (youtube.com). **97:** ""There's So Much I Want To Do": The World According To Zendaya", *Vogue* (vogue.co.uk). **99:** "Tom Holland and Zendaya on the "Ridiculous" Stereotypes About Their Height Difference", SiriusXM (youtube.com). **100:** twitter.com/Timbaland/status/570139965302161408. **101:** "Timothée Chalamet And Zendaya Became "Wonderful Friends"...", *Buzzfeed* (buzzfeed.com); "Why Zendaya's Acrobatic Stunts for 'The Greatest Showman' Are an Awesome Full-Body Workout", *Self* (self.com). **103:** "Zendaya Talks Inspiring Kids to Give Back Via Trick-or-Treat for UNICEF", *The Hollywood Reporter* (hollywoodreporter.com); "Zendaya Talks About Her Works With UNAIDS...", Perez Hilton (youtube.com). **104:** "Tom Holland Comments on the "Tom Holland Umbrella Law"", Entertainment Weekly (youtube.com); "Tom Holland and Zendaya Argue Over The Internets Biggest Debates", LADbible TV (youtube.com); "Zendaya Is Still In Awe Of Tom Holland's Viral 'Umbrella' Lip-Sync Battle", *Esquire* (esquire.com). **105:** "Zendaya Answers Personality Revealing Questions", Vanity Fair (youtube.com). **107:** "Zendaya just opened up about her personal reasons for going vegetarian...", *Hello Giggles* (hellogiggles.com); "Zendaya On Being A Vegetarian", Celebrity Observer (youtube.com); "Zendaya Replies to Fans on the Internet", *GQ* (youtube.com). **108:** "Zendaya Speaks Out on Starring in Quentin Tarantino's Kill Bill 3", *Comic Book* (comicbook.com). **109:** "zendaya being a virgo for 10 minutes straight", nami (youtube.com). **111:** "Zendaya Answers Personality Revealing Questions", Vanity Fair (youtube.com); "Welcome to Zollywood", *GQ* (gq.com). **115:** "Zendaya on the Fashion Industry and Her Instagram Influence", Vogue (youtube.com); "Boohoo.com Teams With Zendaya on Curated Collection", *WWD* (wwd.com); "Zendaya Reveals Her Second Tommy x Zendaya Collection Was Inspired by Her Family", *Teen Vogue* (teenvogue.com). **116:** "Pierpaolo Piccioli: 'Zendaya perfectly represents Valentino's values'", *Yahoo! Life* (uk.style.yahoo.com). **117:** "Zendaya's New Song With Prince Royce Has A Twist We Love", *Refinery29* (refinery29.com). **119:** "Watch Me React To My First YouTube Vids", Zendaya (youtube.com); "Zendaya Comes Out With Her Own App", *Teen Vogue* (teenvogue.com). **120:** "Zendaya's Siblings...", *Hollywood Life* (hollywoodlife.com). **123:** "The Real Meaning Of Zendaya's Name", *Nicki Swift* (nickiswift.com); "Zendaya Plays a Game of Pop Quiz", Marie Claire (youtube.com); "zendaya being a virgo for 10 minutes straight", nami (youtube.com). **124:** "24 Hours With Zendaya", *Harper's Bazaar* (harpersbazaar.com); "Zendaya Shares 19 Facts About Herself", Glamour (youtube.com). **125:** "Zac Efron Can't Stop Flirting With Zendaya", Vid Strike (youtube.com); "Zac Efron Reveals His Favorite On-Screen Kiss Was With Zendaya", *Teen Vogue* (teenvogue.com).

Editor Florence Ward
Designer Isabelle Merry
Senior Production Editor Marc Staples
Senior Production Controller Louise Minihane
Managing Editor Pete Jorgensen
Managing Art Editor Jo Connor
Publishing Director Mark Searle

Written by Satu Hämeenaho-Fox
Cover and interior illustrations Sarah Madden
All illustrations © Sarah Madden 2023

DK would like to thank Madeleine Pollard
for proofreading.

First American Edition, 2023
Published in the United States by DK Publishing
1745 Broadway, 20th Floor, New York, NY 10019

Page design copyright © 2023
Dorling Kindersley Limited
DK, a Division of Penguin Random House LLC
23 24 25 26 27 10 9 8 7 6 5 4 3 2 1
001–335579–Jun/2023

Published in Great Britain
by Dorling Kindersley Limited

A catalog record for this book
is available from the Library of Congress.
ISBN 978-0-7440-8163-3

DK books are available at special discounts when
purchased in bulk for sales promotions, premiums,
fund-raising, or educational use. For details,
contact: DK Publishing Special Markets,
1745 Broadway, 20th Floor, New York, NY 10019
SpecialSales@dk.com

Printed and bound in China

For the curious
www.dk.com

MIX
Paper | Supporting
responsible forestry
FSC™ C018179

This book was made with Forest
Stewardship Council™ certified
paper – one small step in DK's
commitment to a sustainable future.
**For more information go to
www.dk.com/our-green-pledge**